Since You're UP!

Like most people, we enjoy eating. Trying new recipes and being comforted by the old family favorites added excitement and joy to our lives. While the food was always important, the thing we savored the most was those wonderful times in Mammy & Pappy's kitchen, where we all laughed and sang and danced and told our own stories. On these occasions, the meal on the table was always secondary to the quality of time we spent together.

All recipes in this book are taken from family archives. Any resemblance to any other recipes, living or dead, is coincidental.

Copyright ©2005 by ThomasMax Publishing. All rights reserved. No part of this work may be reproduced, stored or transmitted in any form or by any means without written consent of ThomasMax Publishing.

First printing, February 2005.

Cover design by Preston Ward and Lee Clevenger
Front and rear cover photos by Preston Ward
Cover models: Lauren Crews Mozingo and Joseph Alexander Mozingo.
Photos inside depict:
Pages 1 and 11: Pappy
Page 36: Ernest (disguised as Carrotman)
Page 43: Leslie, Lauren, Trey & Pappy
Page 57: Lauren
Page 71: (from left) Robert, Linda, Lauren, Pappy, Mammy, Leslie, Tommy, Brenda & Trey
Page 95: Mammy & Pappy

ISBN No. 0-9764052-1-0

ThomasMax Publishing
P.O. Box 250054
Atlanta, GA 30325
thomasmax.com
404-794-6588

To Pappy…..Who taught us to enjoy good food and good times, but most of all showed us amazing love.

Table of Contents

Pappysnacks................................. Page 1

Appetizers and snacks

This 'n' That............................Page 11

Sauces, soups, salad dressings, vegetables, relishes, and all the et cetera that makes up the name "this 'n' that"

Shonuff Good Stuff......................Page 43

Entrees, meats, main courses

Cookin' for a Crowd......................Page 71

When you need to feed a hungry mob!

Pappylicious...............................Page 95

Because no meal is complete without its just desserts

PAPPY SNACKS

Pappy's greatest love was his family but he sure enjoyed spending time at his lake house! In the fall of the year, he spent long weekends hunting with his son and grandson. He got great pleasure finding new ways to prepare venison for the guys — he also loved to try and trick the ladies into believing they were eating something other than 'Bambi'. Even when you knew what he was doing, you found yourself trying hard to be worthy of the smile he had on his face. He was a true 'Chef' and I am so grateful to have been one of the fortunate ones who enjoyed many wonderful meals and moments with him.

-Brenda Simmons Ward

VENISON SALAMI

5	lbs deer
¾	lb beef fat
6	rounded teaspoons salt cure
2-1/2	teaspoons mustard seed
1	teaspoons Cajun seasoning
1-1/2	teaspoons coarse black pepper
1-1/2	teaspoons chopped garlic
2	teaspoons hickory salt cure

Mix all together thoroughly. Refrigerate in air tight container. Remove each day for three days and remix each day. On 4th day mix and divide into parts. Form roll. Bake at 175° until internal temperature is 152°---about 4 hours. Let cool. Refrigerate. May be frozen.

VENISON JERKY

Slice venison into thin strips. Layer in glass dish. Sprinkle each side with Cajun seasoning and garlic powder. Mix equal parts of soy sauce, Worcestershire sauce, and wine. Cover venison and refrigerate overnight. Hang strips in oven and bake at 125° until dry.

HUSH PUPPIES

1	cup cornmeal
½	cup plain flour
½	teaspoon salt
1	teapoon baking powder
1	egg
	milk
	chopped onion

Mix all together while adding enough milk to be able to drop mixture from spoon. Drop into oil and fry until golden brown.

Since You're UP!

FRIED APPLE PIES

1	package dried apples
1	teaspoon cinnamon
1	tablespoon butter
¼	cup sugar
1	can biscuits

Cook dried apples with cinnamon, butter and sugar. Set aside. Roll out biscuits and put apples in center of each biscuit. Crimp edges and then fry until golden brown.

HORSE RADISH HAM FILLING

2	4-1/2 oz. cans deviled ham
1	stalk celery minced
1	tablespoon prepared horse radish
2	tablespoons mayonnaise

Combine all ingredients and mix well.

SPINACH SQUARES

2	tablespoons margarine melted and divided
1	cup milk
3	eggs
1	cup all purpose flour
1	teaspoon baking powder
¾	teaspoon salt
½	teaspoon dried oregano
¼	teaspoon pepper
¼	teaspoon dried basil
¼	teaspoon thyme
2	10 oz. packages frozen spinach, chopped drained and squeezed dry
2	cups shredded cheddar cheese
2	cups Monterey Jack cheese
1	cup chopped onion

Brush the bottom and side of a 13x9x2 baking dish with 1 tablespoon melted butter. In mixing bowl, combine butter and next nine ingredients. Mix well. Stir in spinach, cheeses, and onions. Spread in baking dish and bake uncovered at 350° for 30 – 35 minutes or until a toothpick near center comes out clean and edges are slightly brown. Cut into squares.

Since You're UP!

WHITE TRASH

1	package pretzels (10 oz. min.)
5	cups Cheerios
5	cups Corn Chex
2	cups salted peanuts
1	pound M&M's
2	packages 12 oz. vanilla chips
3	tablespoons oil

In a large bowl, mix first 5 ingredients. Heat chips and oil for 2 minutes. Pour over Ingredients in bowl and mix well. Spread on wax paper. Let cool. Break apart.

PAPPY'S PARMESAN BITES

1	package 8 oz. cream cheese
1-1/4	cups Kraft Grated Parmesan cheese(divided)
2	cans Crescent dinner rolls
1	cup chopped red pepper
¼	cup chopped fresh parsley

Mix cream cheese and 1 cup of the parmesan cheese with electric mixer on medium speed until well blended. Separate crescent rolls into 8 rectangles. Press perforations together to seal. Spread 3 tablespoons cream cheese mixture on each rectangle. Top with red pepper and parsley. Fold long end of dough up over filling to center. Fold up again to enclose remaining filling. Cut each into 4 equal size squares. Place seam side down on cookie sheet. Sprinkle with remaining ¼ cup parmesan cheese. Bake at 350° for 13 to 15 minutes or until golden brown.

TURKEY CHEESE BALL

1	8 oz. package cream cheese
1	6 oz. blue cheese
1	lb. N.Y. State sharp cheese
1	lb. cheddar sharp cheese
1/8	teaspoon garlic salt
1	tablespoon Worcestershire sauce
2	tablespoons grated onion
1/8	teaspoon monosodium glutamate
2	cups chopped turkey
	Parsley flakes
	Chopped nuts

Grate all cheeses and cream together. Add Worcestershire, onion, garlic and monosodium glutamate. Add turkey and mix all ingredients well. Divide in 2 portions and then roll in parsley flakes and chopped nuts.

Since You're UP!

BLACK BEAN DIP

1	8 oz. cream cheese
1	can black beans (drained)
1	jar peach salsa
1	cup cheddar cheese
1	cup Monterey Jack cheese

Spread cream cheese in a round cooking pan. Pour one can of drained black beans over cream cheese. Pour peach salsa on top of black beans. Top with cheddar and Monterey Jack cheeses. Cook in oven at 350° until cheese melts.

SPINACH DIP

1	pint sour cream
1	cup mayonnaise
1	can water chestnuts chopped fine
1	grated onion
1	package Knorr vegetable soup mix
1	package frozen spinach---cooked chopped and drained.

Combine all ingredients. Hollow out a round loaf of bread and pour mixture in.

Since You're UP!

Since You're UP!

Since You're UP!

In the kitchen with Pappy was an adventure. Not always known for using precise measurements, Pappy would hold out his big hand, shake into his palm whatever seasoning he was using, proclaim it to be just about right and throw it in the pot. To this day, I can't get some of his measurements just right, I guess my hand is not quite big enough!

One of my favorite memories of Pappy's cooking was watching him barbeque chicken. With the open fire just right, the chicken nestled tight on his handmade racks, his own *special sauce* applied at just the right time, he began the long process of turning ordinary chicken into an extraordinary meal! The aroma was wonderful. The chicken even better!

If we had a dollar for every time we heard the words, "Tom, are you going to mess up every pot in the kitchen?" we could all retire now. Pappy was a very messy cook, but some claim that is the mark of genius.

-**Linda Ward Wilson**

Since You're UP!

PAPPY'S HOME MADE BARBEQUE SAUCE

Chicken Stock (make first)

6	chicken (or beef) bouillon cubes
3	cups water
2	whole sticks of margarine

Combine above in pot and bring to a boil.

Mix the following spices in a bowl:
- 3 tablespoons chili powder
- 1 tablespoon paprika
- 2 tablespoons oregano
- 1 rounded teaspoon garlic powder
- 1 rounded teaspoon cayenne pepper
- 2 tablespoons minced dried onion
- 2 tablespoons dried parsley
- 1 teaspoon black pepper
- 2 tablespoons salt

Set aside.

Add the following to the chicken stock:
- ½ cup soy sauce
- 2 tablespoons Worcestershire sauce

Once the chicken stock is boiling, add the spices mixed together earlier in a bowl.

Recipe continues on page 14

Then add:

| 2 | quarts mustard, save jars |

Put :

| 3 | cups vinegar in mustard jars and shake. |

Then put into chicken stock.

Mix the following and then pour into chicken stock:

2	cups ketchup (or 28oz. if you prefer)
1	cup water
2/3	cup sugar

Stir until boiling. Stirring constantly, continue boiling for a good 5 minutes. Let cool and bottle as you desire.

ORANGE GELATIN SALAD

2	packages orange gelatin
1	8 oz. cottage cheese
1	large cool whip
½	cup chopped pecans
1	large can crushed pineapple, drained

Mix all ingredients and refrigerate before serving.

Since You're UP!

PICKLED BEETS

3	cans whole beets
1	cup sugar
1	cup vinegar
2	cups beet juice
1	tablespoon pickling spice

Bring all to a boil except beets. Once boiling, add beets. Bring back to a boil for 5 minutes. Turn off and let set until cool.

PICKLED PEACHES

3	cans whole peaches
1	cup sugar
1	cup vinegar
2	cups peach juice
1	tablespoon pickling spice

Bring all to a boil except peaches. Once boiling, add peaches. Bring back to a boil for 5 minutes. Turn off and let set until cool.

GRAPE WINE

2   gallons smashed grapes
3   gallon water

After two rises, wait one day and strain.
Add three pounds sugar to one gallon of juice. Let stand for 10 days. Strain and bottle, but do not gap tight.

GRAPE JUICE WINE

2   cans frozen grape juice
5   cups sugar
¼   teaspoon dry yeast
¼   cup lukewarm water

Add above to gallon jug. Fill with warm water. Let set 5 weeks.

DIRTY RICE

2	cups rice
4	tablespoons bacon fat
4	tablespoons flour
2	medium chopped onions
1	cup chopped celery
2	cloves crushed garlic
½	lb. ground beef
½	lb. grounded pork
1	beef bouillon cube
1	cup water
2	dried red peppers cut up
½	teaspoon Worcestershire sauce
½	teaspoon hot sauce
	Salt
	Pepper

Cook rice. Heat bacon fat and flour over medium heat till well blended. Add onions, celery, and garlic. When brown, add ground meats and brown well. Stir in bouillon cube dissolved in water, red peppers, Worcestershire sauce, hot sauce, salt and pepper. Cook slowly for 10 minutes. Do not allow mix to get too thick. Mix with rice. Serve hot.

SPINACH & BLACKEYED PEA SALAD

1	package fresh spinach (4 cups)
1	cup cherry tomatoes, halved
2	tablespoons oil, olive preferred
1	red onion sliced
1	tablespoon & teaspoon sugar
2	tablespoons minced garlic
¾	teaspoon dried thyme
½	teaspoon salt
¼	teaspoon pepper
1	can, 15 oz., black-eyed peas, drained & rinsed
2	tablespoons cider vinegar

In serving bowl, combine spinach with cherry tomatoes and set aside. In non stick skillet, heat over medium-high heat. Add onion, sugar, garlic, thyme, salt and pepper. Cook, stirring occasionally until onion softens slightly about 2 minutes. Stir in black-eyed peas. Cook, stirring occasionally, until mixture is heated throughout about 4 or 5 minutes. Remove from heat and stir in vinegar. Add to spinach mixture and toss to combine. Serve immediately.

SALMON CANAPES

1	7-1/2 oz. red salmon, drained, skin and bones removed
2	tablespoons minced celery
2	tablespoons minced green onions with tops
3	tablespoons mayonnaise
1/2	teaspoon lemon juice
1/4	teaspoon salt
1/8	teaspoon pepper
1/8	teaspoon liquid smoke (optional)

Mix salmon, onions and celery. Add mayonnaise, lemon juice, salt and pepper. (and liquid smoke, if you use) Mix well. Cover and chill at least one hour. Serve with cracker or rye bread.

CRABMEAT FILLING

2	oz. blue cheese crumbled
2	tablespoons butter or margarine
1	7-1/2 oz. can of crabmeat, drained and chopped
1	green onion
1	whole pimento chopped

Combine and mix well.

Since You're UP!

DEVILED EGG FILLING

4	chopped eggs
2	tablespoons mayonnaise
2	teaspoons mustard
1	teaspoon dill weed
1	teaspoon salt
¼	teaspoon pepper

Combine and mix well.

CORNMEAL CREPES

1	cup flour
½	cup yellow cornmeal
1-1/2	cup milk
3	eggs
	dash salt
	oil

Combine flour, cornmeal, milk, eggs and salt. Beat with rotary beater until smooth. For each crepe, pour ¼ cup batter into lightly oiled crepe pan or small frying pan. Tilt pan to coat bottom evenly. Cook over medium heat until top is dull and underside is browned. Turn. Cook 10 to 15 seconds.

BAKED BEANS

1 lb. dried beans
1 teaspoon salt

Cook beans until tender.

Sauce:

2 tablespoons oil
1 cup chopped onion
1 cup catsup
½ cup light brown sugar
1 tablespoon Worcestershire sauce
1 teaspoon salt
½ teaspoon dry mustard

Heat oil and add onions. Cook until tender. Add catsup, brown sugar, Worcestershire, salt, dry mustard and 1 cup water. Bring to a boil and cook for 5 minutes. Preheat oven to 350°. Drain beans and save ¼ cup liquid to add to sauce. Combine beans and sauce. Cover and cook 1 hour. Franks can be added and cook for an additional 20 minutes.

SQUASH CASSEROLE

2	cups yellow squash
1/4	cup onion chopped
1/2	cup evaporated milk
1	tablespoon sugar
1	tablespoon butter
1	egg, beaten
1/3	cup grated cheddar cheese
1/2	cup breadcrumbs
	salt/pepper to taste

Cook squash and onion together in small amount of water. Cool and drain. Add beaten egg, milk, sugar, salt and pepper. Butter bottom of dish and add squash mixture. Top with bread crumbs and cheese. Bake at 350° for 35 minutes.

Since You're UP!

FRIED OKRA

1	lb. of okra, sliced
1	cup cornmeal
	dash of salt/pepper
	vegetable oil

Coat okra with cornmeal, salt and pepper. Fry until golden brown.

PAPPY'S CANDIED SWEET POTATOES

3	large sweet potatoes
1-1/2	cups sugar
2	tablespoons flour
	dash of salt
4	tablespoons of butter
½	cup water
1	teaspoon lemon flavoring

Mix sugar, flour and salt and sprinkle over sliced potatoes. Put butter on top. Add lemon flavoring to water and pour over potatoes. Cover with foil and bake at 350° for one hour.

FRIED SQUASH

	squash (sliced)
½	cup milk
1	egg
2	cups chicken breading
	vegetable oil

In bowl, mix egg and milk until even. Put breading in plastic bag. Place sliced squash in egg/milk mix, cover evenly. Take squash and put in bag and shake. Place breaded squash into heated oil and fry until golden brown on both sides.

CABBAGE a la PAPPY

1	cabbage
1	onion
1-2	slices fatback
3	tablespoons butter
	salt/pepper/water

Use all of cabbage that you can, especially the really green leaves. Chop cabbage or shred with your hands. Put cabbage in cooking pot and add ½" water. Add salt and pepper. Take slices of fatback and fry until done. Add onions to fatback and then pour onions, fatback and fatback grease to cabbage. If possible, refrigerate for a couple of hours. Cook, bring water to a boil and then simmer to desired consistency of cabbage.

Since You're UP!

THE MULE SANDWICH

Fried thick bologna with
1 slice onion and **chili** served
on a **hamburger bun**.

CHILI FOR A MULE

¼ - ½	**lb. ground meat**
1	**small onion**
1-2	**tablespoons mustard**
1-2	**tablespoons catsup**
2-5	**tablespoons water**

To taste:
> **chili powder**
> **salt**
> **pepper**
> **paprika**

Cook ground meat until well done. Add onions. Drain grease, if any. Add 2-5 tablespoons water, mustard, catsup, and above spices to taste. Heavy on the chili powder. Bring mixture to a boil, let simmer and adjust to taste. Add more water if needed. Also great on hamburgers and hot dogs!

PAPPY'S OLD TIME RELISH

2	gallon tomatoes
16	ears corn
2	cups okra
2	cups lima beans
3	bell peppers
2	pods hot pepper
3	medium onions
1	cup sugar
½	cup salt
1	cup vinegar

Precook lima beans until done. Precook corn until done. Mix all ingredients except corn and cook for 20 minutes. Add corn and cook for 10 minutes more. Seal in hot jars.

Since You're UP!

CHOW-CHOW-CHOW -DOWN RELISH

4	cups chopped cabbage
3	cups chopped cauliflower
2	cups chopped green tomatoes
2	cups chopped onions
2	cups chopped green peppers
1	cup chopped sweet red peppers
3	tablespoons canning salt
2-1/2	cups white house vinegar
1-1/2	cups sugar
2	teaspoons celery seed
2	teaspoons dry mustard
1	teaspoon mustard seed
1	teaspoon ground turmeric
½	teaspoon ground ginger

Combine chopped vegetables, sprinkle with salt. Let stand 4 to 6 hours in a cool place. Drain well. Combine vinegar, sugar, spices and simmer 10 minutes. Add vegetables and simmer 10 minutes more bringing to a boil. Carefully ladle relish into hot jars leaving ¼" headspace.

PAPPY'S PICKLE HOT PEPPER (BETTER THAN PETER PIPER'S)

2	parts water
1	part vinegar
1	teaspoon celery seed
1	teaspoon mustard seed
1	teaspoon turmeric
6	bay leaves
2	garlic cloves
	Hot peppers
	salt
	oil

Bring all above to a boil, except peppers and salt. Clean and salt peppers. Set aside. Put one bay leaf and one garlic clove at the bottom of each jar then pack peppers in jar. Add one teaspoon oil per jar. Add mixture and refrigerate overnight.

SWEET CHOW CHOW

1	tablespoon whole mustard seed
1	tablespoon turmeric
2	cups sugar
1	quart vinegar

Add desired vegetables and bring to a boil for 15 minutes and seal in hot jars.

CORN RELISH

½	cup vinegar
1/3	cup sugar
½	teaspoon celery seed
½	teaspoon mustard seed
¼	teaspoon hot sauce
1	16-oz. can whole kernel corn, drained
2	tablespoons bell pepper
1	tablespoon pimento
1	tablespoon onion

Combine 1st 6 ingredients and bring to a boil. Cook 2 minutes. Cool. Combine remaining ingredients and then pack into hot jars.

RAISIN SAUCE

1	cup raisins
1-1/2	cups water
1	cup jelly
1-1/2	cup orange juice
6	tablespoons brown sugar
3	tablespoons corn starch
	Dash all spice

Mix all ingredients and bring to a boil.

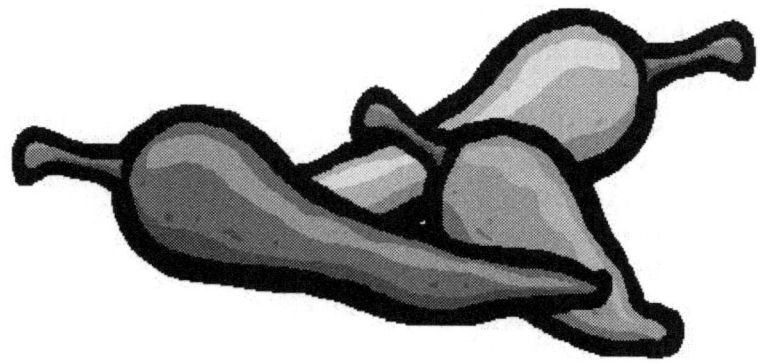

PAPPY'S HOT PEPPER SAUCE

12	green hot peppers
12	red hot peppers
14	large onions
7	green/yellow tomatoes
3	cups cabbage
3	cups sugar
5	cups vinegar
3	teaspoons salt

Coarse grind or chop peppers or onions. When handling peppers, do not use bare hands. Put in large post. Add sugar, vinegar, and salt. Coarse grind or chop green tomatoes and cabbage. Add to peppers and onions. Bring to a boil and cook slowly for 30 minutes. Put in pint sized sterilized jars and seal. Yield: 12-14 pints.

TACO SEASONING BLEND

12 or 3	tablespoons chili powder
4 or 1	tablespoons salt
4 or 1	tablespoons garlic powder
6 or 1-1/2	½ teaspoons black pepper
3 or ¾	teaspoon red pepper

Mix and store in an air tight container. Good with beef or chicken.

PAPPY'S SWEET & SPICY MUSTARD

5	tablespoons dry mustard
½	cup sugar
1	tablespoon all purpose flour
½	teaspoon salt
	dash red pepper
2	eggs, beaten
½	cup vinegar
1	tablespoon butter or margarine

Combine mustard, sugar, flour salt, and red pepper in top of double boiler. Add eggs and vinegar and blend thoroughly. Place over boiling water and cook while stirring constantly until thickened. Add butter and stir until melted. Cool mixture and store in the refrigerator.

Since You're UP!

BROCCOLI AND CAULIFLOWER DRESSING

½   cup mayonnaise
¼   cup salad/vegetable oil
1/3   cup vinegar
1/3   cup sugar
        salt/pepper

Mix all ingredients and pour over broccoli and cauliflower pieces and refrigerate. Can be multiplied.

Since You're UP!

PAPPY'S SALAD DRESSING

2/3	cup oil
½	cup vinegar
2	tablespoons lemon juice
1/3	cup catsup
1/3	cup brown sugar
1/3	cup white sugar
1	teaspoon salt
2	teaspoons paprika
2	tablespoons grated onion
1	teaspoon celery seed
1	garlic clove, chopped.

Combine all ingredients in a jar and shake well. Let stand 24 hours.

SLAW DRESSING

½	cup mayonnaise
¼	cup vegetable oil
1/3	cup vinegar
1/3	cup sugar
	salt/pepper

Mix together, pour over chopped cabbage and chill.

BROCCOLI NOODLE SLAW

1	bag broccoli slaw mix
1	small purple onion
1	small bell pepper
2	packs Ramen Noodle Soup (chicken)
½	cup oil
½	cup vinegar
½	cup sugar

Mix sugar, vinegar, and oil. Then break apart the noodles and add the packet of chicken flavoring and mix well. Let mixture set while cutting the pepper and onion and mix them all together. Add the broccoli slaw mix and stir well. Put in covered container and let stand overnight.

BBQ SLAW

1	head cabbage, grated
1	tablespoon mayonnaise
1	tablespoon mustard
1	tablespoon Worcestershire sauce
1	tablespoon A-1 steak sauce
1	tablespoon sugar
1	tablespoon vinegar
½	bottle catsup
2	shakes hot sauce
1	teaspoon chili powder

Salt and pepper to taste.

Mix above ingredients and serve with BBQ.

PAPPY'S PASTA SALAD

1	lb. pasta, cooked
1	cup thinly sliced zucchini
1	cup broccoli
½	cup green peppers
½	cup red peppers
½	cup shredded carrots
½	cup black pitted olives
	thin strips of salami
	cheddar cheese

Dressing for Pasta salad:

1	cup undiluted Carnation milk
4-6	tablespoons vinegar
1	cup salad oil
1	teaspoon Italian seasoning
4	tablespoons grated parmesan cheese
1	tablespoon garlic salt
2	tablespoons sugar

Combine in jar and shake well.

Mix pasta salad and dressing and chill.

Since You're UP!

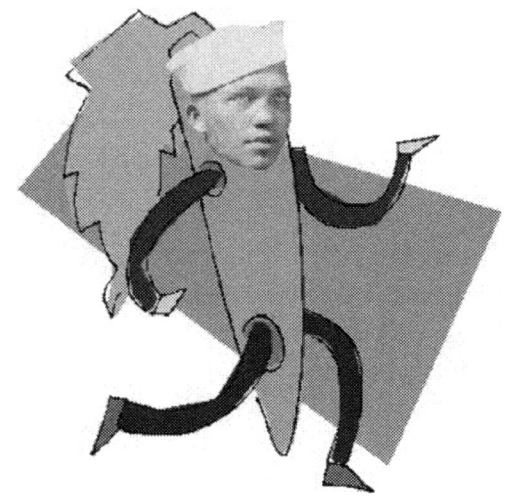

MARINATED VEGETABLES

1	bunch fresh broccoli
1	lb. fresh mushrooms
1	head cauliflower
1	cup cider vinegar
1	tablespoon sugar
1	tablespoon dill weed
1	tablespoon Accent
1	teaspoon salt
1	teaspoon pepper
1	teaspoon garlic salt
1-1/2	cup vegetable oil

Wash vegetables and cut broccoli and cauliflower into small pieces. Mix remaining ingredients. Pour over vegetables. Cover and refrigerate for 24 hours. Baste from time to time. Drain and serve.

Since You're UP!

DRAYTON STREET SOUP

1	lb. ground beef
1	onion, chopped
4	cups water
1	16 oz. can tomatoes
2	beef bouillon cubes
1	teaspoon salt
1	teaspoon pepper
1	bay leaf
¾	cup celery, chopped
1	tablespoon Worcestershire sauce
1	10 oz. package frozen vegetables
2	cups noodles
	dash of thyme

Brown beef and onion, set aside. Bring the tomatoes, water, bouillon cubes, salt and pepper to a boil. Add celery and vegetables. Boil until tender. Add noodles and simmer until done. Add beef, onion, Worcestershire sauce and thyme. Cook 10 to 15 minutes longer.

CREAM OF BROCCOLI SOUP

1	cup chopped celery
2	cups chopped onions
2	10 oz. chopped broccoli
2	cups cottage cheese
4	cups milk
4	cans cream of chicken soup(undiluted)
1	teaspoon salt
¼	teaspoon pepper

Cream cottage cheese and milk. Add to cooked vegetables and heat.

PAPPY'S TATER SOUP

½	cup diced celery
½	cup diced carrots
½	cup diced onions
2	tablespoons margarine
2	tablespoons all purpose flour
1	quart milk
2	chicken bouillon cubes
2	tablespoons minced parsley
½	teaspoon salt
½	teaspoon seasoned salt
¼	teaspoon cayenne pepper
6	medium potatoes(peeled, cubed and cooked until tender)

In a pot sauté celery, carrot and onions in margarine until tender. Stir in flour until smooth. Gradually add milk, cook and stir until bubbly and thick. Add bouillon cubes, salt, seasoned salt, and cayenne and simmer for 20 minutes stirring occasionally. Divide the potatoes and mash one half. Add all to soup. Simmer for 20 minutes until heated through.
Garnish at your desire: bacon bits/chives/cheese.

VEGETABLE SOUP

2	large potatoes, peeled, wedged, cooked and drained
½	lb. hamburger, browned and drained
2	cans veg-all
2	cans okra and tomatoes
1	small can lima beans
1	small can of corn
1	small can of peas
1	small can of green beans
1	small can of tomato sauce

Let all ingredients come to a boil and then simmer for 15-30 minutes.

GARDEN VEGETABLE BEEF SOUP

2	packs Knorr vegetable soup mix
2	lbs. stew beef
15	fresh tomatoes, peeled and wedged
1	large onion, chopped
3	pieces celery, chopped
5	potatoes, peeled and wedged
2	cups fresh green beans, snapped
2	cups fresh corn off the cob
2	cups fresh carrots, chopped
2	cups fresh okra, chopped
1	can peas
1	small tomato paste
3-5	cups water

Salt and pepper to taste

Brown stew beef until done and set aside. Combine soup mix and water and start to cook in a big cooking pot. Add the remainder of the ingredients and bring to a slow boil and then cook on low for 2 hours.

Since You're UP!

My grandfather meant the world to me. My father died when I was young, and it was my grandfather and uncle who stepped up to fill the role of 'Dad'.

My mom worked during the week and I was fortunate to spend my days with my grandparents, Mammy and Poppa. I can remember my mom dropping me off at their house early in the morning and even through sleepy eyes I can remember my grandfather's sweet smile. I often found him in the kitchen awaiting my arrival just so we could cook breakfast together. And this wasn't just cereal or pancakes, but it was sausage and gravy with biscuits. They were the best. This was the way I spent countless mornings.

Time has passed and I have grown up. Yet I still make our special sausage and gravy with biscuits and I know that Poppa is standing there in the kitchen with me. He lives in my heart and in my memories. It is his smile and laughter that you see through me on the mornings when I make this special breakfast.

-**Lauren Crews Mozingo**

RISE 'N' SHINE BISCUITS WITH LAUREN'S GRAVY

2 ½	cups self rising flour
2	teaspoons baking powder
2	tablespoons powered sugar
1/3	cup Crisco
1	cup buttermilk

Mix all ingredients well, roll and cut.
Melt one stick butter and dip each biscuit. Bake at 400° until done.

Crumble ground sausage
Flour
Milk
Salt/pepper

Fry sausage until done. Do not drain all of the grease. Add flour, salt, pepper, and milk. Start out using a little flour and milk until you get consistency you want. Bring to a bubble boil, stirring constantly. Then serve over biscuits.

Artwork by Lauren Crews Mozingo, age 4.

PAPPY'S CASSEROLE

1	pound ground beef
½	cup chopped onion (more if you prefer)
1	can cream of celery soup
	salt/pepper to taste
1	bag frozen tater tots (average size)
	shredded cheese (sharp)

Take one pound ground beef (raw) and press down (like a pie crust) in a 9x9 rectangular baking dish. Sprinkle onions over meat and salt and pepper to taste. Spread non diluted cream of celery soup over ground beef and onions. Sprinkle a thin layer of cheese. Cover top with tater tots. Sprinkle another layer of cheese. Cook at 350° for 1 hour.

TATER 'N' BEEF CASSEROLE

1	pound ground chuck
1	medium onion
1	10 ½ oz. cream of mushroom soup
	salt/pepper to taste
	sliced raw potatoes
½	cup milk

Brown ground beef, drain. Mix ground beef, chopped onions, and soup. Layer 1/3 mixture in bottom of pan. Top with thin sliced potatoes. Sprinkle with salt and pepper. Top with remaining meat mixture. Pour milk over top. Cover with foil for half of cooking time. Then uncover and cook until potatoes are tender and top is brown. Bake at 350° for 1 hour 15 minutes.

HAMBURGER SALAMI

5	pounds hamburger
5	rounded teaspoons salt cure
2 ½	teaspoons mustard seed
2 ½	teaspoons coarse black pepper
2 ½	teaspoons garlic salt
1	teaspoon hickory salt

Mix all together thoroughly. Refrigerate in air tight container. Remove each day for three days and remix. On fourth day remove and divide in 4 parts. Knead and form in roll. Bake 8 hours at 175°. Turn after 4 hours. Let cool and refrigerate for 10 days. May be frozen.

SPEEDY CASSEROLE

5	slices bacon cut into ½ inch pieces
1	cup chopped onions
1	cup sliced carrots
1	pound kielbasa cut into 1 inch slices
½	pound boneless chicken breast cut into 1 inch slices
¼	cup dry white wine
2	cans (16 oz. each) small white beans (drained)
1	can tomatoes (16 oz.) drained and chopped
¾	cup beef broth
1	tablespoon Worcestershire sauce
1	tablespoon basil
¼	teaspoon thyme

In a large skillet, cook bacon over medium high heat. Remove with slotted spoon and drain on paper towels. Add onions and carrots to the bacon grease in skillet. Sautee until golden brown. Remove with slotted spoon and set aside. Add kielbasa and chicken to skillet and cook until slightly brown. Remove and set aside. Pour off remainder of grease in skillet. Then pour wine into skillet and heat to boiling. Return all ingredients to skillet and simmer for 10 minutes.

FIESTA CREPES EN CASSEROLE

2	pounds ground beef
½	cup finely chopped onion
½	cup chopped celery
1	can (17 oz.) cream style corn
2	cans (8 oz.) tomato sauce
1	envelope (1 ½ oz.) taco seasoning mix
4	oz. cheddar cheese (shredded)
1/3	cup sliced ripe olives
	crepes

Brown ground beef, onion and celery in large skillet. Pour off drippings. Combine tomato sauce and taco seasoning mix until blended. Add 1 1/3 cups tomato sauce mixture to corn and mix well. Spoon 2 tablespoons meat mixture into each crepe. Roll to close. Spread remaining mixture into a 13 X 9 baking dish. Place crepes seam side down on top of meat. Spoon remaining tomato sauce over crepes. Bake 20 minutes at 375°. Sprinkle with cheese and top with olives.

CHEESEBURGER PIE

1	pound ground beef
1	cup chopped onion
½	teaspoon salt
1	cup shredded cheese
1	cup milk
½	cup Bisquick
2	eggs

Grease 9 inch pie baking dish. Cook ground beef and onion until done and brown. Stir in salt. Spread mixture into pie baking dish and sprinkle with cheese. Mix remaining ingredients with fork until blended then pour over mixture in baking dish. Bake 25 – 30 minutes at 400°.

MAMMY'S MEAT LOAF

1	pound ground beef
1	onion
2	sticks celery
	salt/pepper to taste
2	eggs
	breadcrumbs (1/2 to 1 cup)
	tomato sauce or ketchup (1/2 cup)
	tomato paste

Chop onion and celery. Add all ingredients together except for tomato paste. Shape mixture into a loaf shape and put into a baking dish. Cook ½ time covered. Then remove and uncover and add tomato paste on top of meatloaf and return to oven uncovered. Bake 1 hour at 350°.

ROAST PORK

1 cup apple juice
1 cup pepper jelly
1 cup apple cider vinegar
3-4 pounds pork roast

Glaze mixture: 3/4 cup pepper jelly; 1/4 cup vinegar

Mix first three ingredients and pour over roast. Allow to marinate for at least 8 hours or overnight. 325° for approx. 2 hours. Glaze with mixture of pepper jelly and vinegar.

MAC 'N' CHEESE CROCKPOT

8 oz. macaroni
1/2 stick butter
1 can evaporated milk (tall can)
1 1/2 cups milk
2 eggs
2 teaspoons salt
  Dash dry mustard
3 cups grated cheese

Combine all ingredients and cook on low setting of crock pot for 3 hours.

PAPPY'S PORK HASH

3 ½	pounds Boston Butt Pork roast
1	pound beef round steak
3	medium chopped onions
1	cup prepared mustard
2	tablespoons Worcestershire sauce
½	cup vinegar
1	teaspoon sugar
½	pound butter
6	eggs, boiled and grated (optional)
	Few drops hot pepper sauce
	Salt and pepper to taste

Cut meat into chunks and add onions. Cover with water and cook until very tender, approx. 3 hours. Remove from heat and let cool naturally or add some ice and stir. When cool, pull and shred meat until fine. More water may be needed. Add other ingredients except eggs and bring to a boil. Simmer while stirring often. Add eggs and serve over rice.

BACKALLEY BRUNSWICK STEW

2 ½	pound chicken, cut into pieces
½	cup chopped onions
1	cup quartered tomatoes
1	can (8 oz.) whole peeled tomatoes
1	cup chopped and peeled potatoes
1 ½	cups lima beans (or butter beans)
1 ½	cups corn
1 ½	teaspoon Worcestershire sauce
2	tablespoon ketchup
1	tablespoon mustard
1	tablespoon vinegar
	Salt and pepper to taste
	Few drops of hot sauce.

Cover chicken with water and simmer until tender. Drain chicken and set aside broth. When chicken cools, remove bones and skin and then shred meat. Put broth in a pot. Add tomatoes, onions, potatoes, beans, and corn. Cover and simmer until vegetables are tender. Add shredded meat, Worcestershire, ketchup, mustard, vinegar, salt, pepper and hot sauce. Cover and simmer for 30 minutes.

NORA'S LIVER NIPS

2-3	pounds beef roast
¾	pound beef liver
½	pound suet
1	onion, small and grated
2	eggs, beaten
¼	teaspoon baking powder
½	teaspoon sweet basil
½	teaspoon thyme
2	cups flour
	Salt and pepper to taste

Boil roast until tender, remove roast and save broth for nips. Boil liver in a separate container. Grind liver and suet and add onion. Combine flour, baking powder and seasonings, add liver mixture, add egg and water(beef broth if there is enough). Mix well. Mixture should be a little stiff. Heat broth to simmer, drop nips by teaspoons into simmering broth. Drop slowly so that broth continues to simmer. After all nips are in broth, let simmer briefly.

RED BEANS AND RICE

2	pounds red beans
6	cups water
2	large onions, chopped
4	garlic cloves, minced
1	large green pepper, chopped
1	large red pepper, chopped
½	pound salt pork
1	cup dry red wine
½	cup chopped parsley
½	teaspoon oregano
1	tablespoon Old Bay seasoning
3	bay leaves
1	teaspoon celery seed
1	teaspoon salt
1	teaspoon pepper
½	teaspoon crushed red pepper
½	teaspoon ground red pepper
1	teaspoon hot sauce
2	pounds smoked sausage (1/2" pieces)
2	cans (11 oz.) diced tomatoes and green chilies

Combine first 19 ingredients in a large pot and bring to a boil. Cover, reduce heat and simmer till tender. Add sausage and tomatoes and cook for 30 minutes. Remove salt pork and bay leaves. Serve over rice.

LINDA'S LASAGNA

½	pound lasagna noodles
2	tablespoons olive oil
2	cloves garlic, minced
¼	teaspoon garlic powder
1	medium onion, chopped
1	pound hamburger
1 ½	teaspoon salt
½	teaspoon pepper
½	teaspoon basil
1	tablespoon parsley, minced
2	6 oz. cans tomato paste
1 ½	cup hot boiling water
2	eggs, beaten
1	pint cottage cheese
½	pound mozzarella cheese
¼	cup parmesan cheese

Cook noodles about 15 minutes, then drain. Heat oil; cook garlic and onion until soft. Add beef and seasoning, cook until crumbly. Add tomato paste, hot water and simmer for 5 minutes. Set aside. Blend beaten egg with cottage cheese. In a 13 X 9 X 2 inch baking dish, put a thin layer of meat sauce, half the noodles, all the cottage cheese and egg mixture and half the mozzarella. Repeat with half sauce, rest of noodles and remainder of sauce and mozzarella. Sprinkle with parmesan. Bake at 350° for 30 minutes. Let cool for 10 minutes and serve.

FETTUCCINE

12	oz. fettuccine
1	cup chicken broth
2	garlic cloves minced
1	cup quartered mushrooms
½	cup thinly sliced green onions
4	oz. cream cheese cubed
4	oz. fully cooked ham cubed
1	cup quartered cherry tomatoes
½	cup grated parmesan cheese
¼	teaspoon white pepper

Cook fettuccine according to directions. In saucepan over heat bring broth and garlic to boil. Add mushrooms and onions. Reduce heat and simmer uncovered for 5 minutes or until mushrooms are tender. Add cream cheese and ham. Cook and stir until cheese melts. Add tomatoes and simmer for 5 minutes. Remove from heat and add remaining ingredients.

SPAGHETTI & MEATBALLS

½	lb. ground pork, halved
½	cup oil
1	medium onion, chopped
3	cloves garlic
3	14 oz cans tomatoes
1-1/2	pounds ground chuck
1	egg
½	teaspoon Parmesan cheese
1	teaspoon onion, chopped
½	clove garlic
	salt and pepper (to taste)
	bread crumbs
1	small can tomato paste
1	tsp sugar
½	tsp cayenne pepper

Fry together ¼-pound ground pork, oil, onion and garlic until cooked, not brown. Add 3 cans of tomatoes (if whole, cut up). Cook in 5-quart saucepan slowly for 2 hours. Meanwhile, make meatballs from ground chuck, ¼-pound ground pork, egg, Parmesan cheese, onion, garlic and salt and pepper to taste. Add enough bread crumbs to stiffen for balls. Brown meatballs and drop into sauce after two hours. Then add tomato paste, sugar, cayenne pepper and more salt (to taste). Cook an additional 20 minutes. Spoon over hot spaghetti noodles.

PASTA CARBONARA

1-1/2	pounds bacon, diced
½	cup plus 3 tbsp olive oil
1	large onion, diced
1	large pepper, diced
½	cup chopped mushrooms
	dry white wine
1	12-ounce box fettuccini (green or yellow)
1	stick butter, melted
2	eggs
¾	cup Parmesan and Romano cheeses, grated and mixed
1/3	cup parsley, chopped
	lots of fresh ground pepper

Fry bacon until lightly browned, pour off almost all grease and set aside. In same pan, add 3 tbsps of olive oil and sauté onion, pepper and mushrooms until soft. Return bacon to pan and deglaze with ¾ cup of wine; let simmer 5-10 minutes, always keeping enough wine in pan to keep moist.

In very large pot, boil water. Add a small amount of olive oil and salt to water. When rapidly boiling, add pasta and cook until barely tender. While pasta is boiling, melt butter. In another bowl, beat egg.

Drain pasta quickly but thoroughly in colander and return to warm pot. Immediately add beaten egg, melted butter, cheese, parsley, olive oil, and bacon/vegetable/wine mixture. Stir all together. Sprinkle with pepper.

CHICKEN & NOODLES

2	tablespoons butter
1-1/2	cups sliced carrots
1-1/2	cups broccoli florets
1	cup sliced mushrooms
½	cup sliced red onion
2	cups chopped chicken, uncooked
1-3/4	cups ready-to-serve chicken broth
1 to 2	teaspoons hot pepper sauce
1	cup sour cream
2	tablespoons all purpose flour
1	12-oz package of noodles
	salt and pepper to taste

In a large skillet, melt butter, add carrots and cook 3 minutes. Add remaining vegetables and cook 2 minutes. Add chicken, cook until done. Add broth and pepper sauce and heat thoroughly. Stir together sour cream and flour and add mixture gradually to broth. Heat, stirring constantly. Do not boil. Toss with hot cooked noodles. Add salt and pepper to taste.

CHICKEN & ROTELLE SALAD WITH PESTO DRESSING

1	3-pound broiler fryer, cut up
1	pound rotelle spiral pasta
1	cup olive oil
4	cups fresh parsley leaves
¼	cup pine nuts or walnuts
2	large cloves of garlic, minced
1-1/2	teaspoons leaf basil
1	teaspoon salt
½	cup grated Parmesan cheese
	lettuce leaves
2	cups cherry tomatoes, halved
¼	cup pitted black olives

Simmer chicken in water in covered saucepan until tender. When cool, cut into strips. Cook rotelle according to directions on package. Drain, rinse with cold water, drain again and place into large bowl. Combine olive oil, parsley, pine nuts, garlic, basil and salt in container of electric blender and whirl until parsley is finely chopped. Pour into small bowl, and stir in cheese. Line edge of salad bowl with lettuce leaves. Toss rotelle with half of dressing. Place chicken in center of bowl and edge bowl with tomatoes and olives. Serve at room temperature.

CHICKEN AND DUMPLINGS

1	cup flour (1/2 self-rising; 1/2 plain)
1	pinch salt
1	egg
2	tablespoons cold water (adjust according to size of egg)
	chicken broth

Blend flour, salt, egg and water into ball of dough and roll out on floured cloth. Cut into strips, 1 inch or 1-1/2 inches. Holding strip in left hand, pinch off small pieces and drop into boiling chicken broth. Boil until done (10-15 minutes).

Since You're UP!

MORE CHICKEN AND DUMPLINGS

Meat:
1	hen or fat fryer, cooked
1	can of cream of chicken soup
	salt and pepper

Dumplings:

¾	cup cold broth
1	egg
	small amount of salt and pepper
	plain flour

Sift plain flour; add 1 egg, salt and pepper. Mix together. Knead dough until very stiff. Roll out paper thin; cut into strips, break in pieces. Add to slow rolling boil broth, with chicken soup mixed well and chicken pieces. Use long-handle egg turner; ease around bottom to loosen dough. Cover and cook slowly for 25 minutes. Let set 1 hour before eating.

MOO GOO GAI PAN
(ORIENTAL CHICKEN)

6-8	half chicken breasts, taken off bone
2	eggs
½	tsp powdered ginger
½	cup flour
1	small onion (whole)
¼	cup cornstarch
2	tbsp oil
2	tablespoons white wine or 2 tablespoons vinegar and 1 tablespoon sugar
¼	teaspoon pepper

Combine all ingredients except chicken into sauce. Marinate chicken for 1 hour or more in sauce; bite-size pieces are best.

SWEET & SOUR SAUCE FOR MOO GOO GAI PAN

1/3	cup brown sugar
¼	cup cornstarch
½	cup soy sauce
½	cup vinegar
2	cups chicken stock (boil skin and bone in 2 cups of water)

Combine brown sugar, cornstarch, soy sauce and vinegar. Slowly add chicken broth. Cook until thick. Very hot grease is recommended. Serve over rice.

GINGER CHICKEN

2	whole chicken breasts
¼	lb. fresh mushrooms
1	10-1/2 oz. can condensed chicken broth
½	lb. fresh spinach
1	16-oz. can bean sprouts
1	large onion
2	carrots, sliced into strips
2	tablespoons soy sauce
½	cup sherry
1	teaspoon ginger root
½	teaspoon salt
½	teaspoon ground ginger
2	tablespoons butter
2	tablespoons cornstarch

Slice chicken into ½" strips. Sauté in butter until golden brown. Slice onion and mushrooms and brown. Add carrot strips and chicken broth, soy sauce, ¼ cup sherry, ginger root, salt and ground ginger. Simmer for 15 minutes. Add spinach and bean sprouts. Simmer for 5 minutes, covered. Add corn starch and ¼ cup sherry and cook until thick.

JAPANESE CHICKEN WINGS

- 2   lbs. chicken wings
- ½   cup soy sauce
- ½   cup sake
- ¼   cup sugar
- ¼   teaspoon crushed red pepper
- 1   garlic clove, crushed
- 1-1/2 teaspoons grated fresh ginger root (do NOT use powder)

Cut wings into parts. Mix all ingredients in 12x8 baking dish. Let wings marinate at least 1 hour in mixture in refrigerator. Can be prepared up to 24 hours in advance (turn occasionally). Bake in preheated oven at 375° uncovered for 90 minutes, turning occasionally. Serve warm or cold.

COATED BAKED CHICKEN OR FISH

	Meat, chicken or fish
1/3	cup dry skim milk
2	teaspoons instant chicken bouillon
1	teaspoon dry mustard
1	teaspoon paprika
¼	teaspoon black pepper
	dash of garlic salt (chicken only)
	dash of seasoned salt (fish only)

Mix dry skim milk, bouillon, mustard, paprika and black pepper. Coat meat with mixture. Let stand at least 4 hours. Bake at 350° for 45 minutes or until done. Add garlic salt (chicken) or seasoned salt (fish).

CHICKEN & RICE CASSEROLE

6	slices of bacon cut in thirds
1	cup rice
2	packages of onion soup mix
2	cans of cream of mushroom soup
	salt and pepper
8	chicken legs and thighs
8	ounces sliced mushrooms
3	cups water

Arrange bacon in bottom of pan, sprinkle rice over bacon.

Mix onion soup mix, mushroom soup and 3 cups of water, mix well and pour 1/3 of mixture over rice.

Arrange chicken pieces on top of soup and rice mixture. Sprinkle with salt and pepper. Scatter mushrooms around chicken pieces. Pour remaining soup mixture over chicken.

Cover with foil and bake 1 hour and 15 minutes at 350°.

JUST MARINARA SAUCE

2	28 oz. cans crushed tomatoes (or garden tomatoes if you prefer)
1	can Italian style tomato paste (optional)
1-3	gloves garlic, chopped
	olive oil
	salt
	Oregano to taste
1	Bay leaf
	Italian seasoning to taste

Pour enough olive oil to lightly coat the bottom of your cooking pot. Heat. Take the chopped garlic and put in olive oil. Do not brown garlic. Add seasonings to taste. Stir garlic and seasonings constantly then add one can tomatoes. Stir in tomato paste and then add remaining tomatoes. Bring to a boil then let simmer slowly for 30 – 40 minutes. Serve over pasta. Also very good with meatballs and Italian sausage. Pour the marinara sauce over the cooked meat and pasta. For pure marinara sauce do not cook meat and sauce together. Do not eat bay leaf.

PAPPY'S CHILI IN A POT

1 – 2	pounds ground beef
2	sticks celery, chopped
2	onions, medium, chopped
2 – 3	14 oz can whole tomatoes
1	14 oz. can red kidney beans, drained
1	14 oz. can dark kidney beans, drained
1	green bell pepper, chopped
1	bay leaf
1	tablespoon oregano
3-5	tablespoon chili powder
1	teaspoon mustard powder
2 – 3	cloves garlic, chopped
	Cheddar cheese, shredded
	Sour cream

Brown ground meat until done in a skillet. Drain grease and set meat aside. In a large pot, combine all ingredients, including ground beef, except cheese and sour cream. Bring to a boil and cook on a slow simmer for 30 – 40 minutes. Serve in a bowl and top with cheese and sour cream. Do not eat bay leaf.

Since You're UP!

COOKIN' FOR A CROWD

A good meal begins long before the food gets to the table. One of the most fun things to do with Pappy was to accompany him to the grocery store. Pappy really knew his way around the grocery store. He knew just what he wanted and where to find it---and could always be talked into special treats that were not on the list.

Pappy's love of cooking was only matched by his love of cooking for a crowd. This especially came in handy when he started doing the majority of cooking for our church. He never missed an opportunity to be involved with the church and the weekly cooking for the Wednesday night super and the Thursday cooking for the people who needed a meal that was delivered by the church staff. Of course my participation was the clean up crew...but we all had good fellowship and good food.

-Ramah Livingston Ward

BEEF STEW

30	lbs. stew beef
3	lbs. onions, diced
5	gal. water
¾	cup salt
6	tablespoons pepper
4-1/2	quarts diced tomatoes
4-1/2	quarts catsup
4	# 10 cans Veg-All, drained

In a large pot, combine beef, onions, salt, ½ gallon of water, pepper, tomatoes and catsup. Cook until tender, then add 4-1/2 gallons of water and the Veg-All. Cook an additional 30 minutes and serve hot.

Serves 150.

MEAT LOAF

24	lbs ground chuck
10-1/2	cups rolled oats
¼	cup salt and 3 tablespoons salt
2-1/2	tablespoons black pepper
4	cups onions
2	cups bell pepper (optional)
2	cups celery (optional)
14	eggs
1	# 10 can crushed tomatoes

Combine rolled oats, salt, pepper, onion, bell pepper, celery, eggs (beaten) and tomatoes. Combine with beef and mix well until blended. Put into pam-sprayed loaf pans. Bake at 375° for 30 minutes. Glaze top with glaze sauce (below). Bake an additional one hour (or until well down).

Serves 100.

GLAZE FOR MEAT LOAF

1-1/4	cup catsup
¾	cup mustard
¾	cup brown sugar

Since You're UP!

BEEF TIPS

27	lbs. beef cut into 1" cubes
2-1/2	tablespoons salt
2-1/2	tablespoons pepper
2-1/2	tablespoons dried thyme
20	cans 10-3/4 oz. mushroom soup
5-1/2	cups water
5-1/2	cups chopped onion
¾	cup chopped fresh parsley
3	teaspoons browning sauce

Combine beef, salt, pepper and thyme. Mix well. Place in greased baking pans. Bake uncovered at 400° for 15 minutes. Stir and bake an additional 15 minutes. Drain. Combine soup, water, onion, parsley and browning sauce. Pour equally over beef. Mix well. Cover and bake at 350° for 1-1/2 to 2 hours, until beef is tender. Serve over rice.

Serves: 100 (3/4 cup servings)

PARTY BEEF CASSEROLE

6	tablespoons all-purpose flour
2	teaspoons salt
1	teaspoon black pepper
4	lbs. boneless round cut in ½" cubes
6	tablespoons cooking oil
2	cups water
1	cup beef broth
2	cloves garlic
1	cup chopped onion
1	teaspoon dried thyme
½	teaspoon dried rosemary (crushed)
4	cups sliced mushrooms
4	cups frozen peas
6	cups mashed potatoes

Combine flour, salt and pepper in plastic bag. Add beef and shake to coat beef. Add cooking oil to skillet and brown beef. Place beef and drippings in a greased baking pan. To skillet, add water and beef broth, garlic, onion, thyme and rosemary. Bring to boil, simmer uncovered for 5 minutes. Stir in mushrooms. Pour over meat mixture and mix well. Cover. Bake at 350° for 1-1/2 hours, until beef is tender. Sprinkle peas over meat and mix. Spread potatoes evenly over the top. Brush with butter, sprinkle with paprika. Bake for 15-20 minutes.

Serves 20

Since You're UP!

SLOPPY JOES

20	lbs. ground beef
4	large onions, chopped
4	large green peppers, chopped
4	cups chopped celery
1	cup packed brown sugar
4	cups catsup
24	oz. tomato paste
4	15-ounce cans tomato sauce
6-8	cups water
1	cup vinegar
2/3	cup Worcestershire sauce
100	buns

In a large pot, brown beef, onions, celery and pepper in batches until meat is brown. Remove with slotted spoon to another pot. Add remainder of ingredients (except buns). Cover and simmer for 3 to 4 hours. Serve on buns.

Serves: 100 sandwiches

CHICKEN PIE DELUXE

2	cups chopped onions
2-1/2	sticks margarine
8	cups flour
12	cups chicken broth
8	cups chopped chicken
2	cups chopped carrots, cooked
2	cups cooked peas
2	teaspoons salt
1	teaspoon pepper
4	teaspoons dried tarragon
½	teaspoon cayenne pepper
8	teaspoons baking powder
1	dozen eggs
3	cups milk

(1) In large pan, cook onions until soft in two sticks of margarine. Add 2 cups flour, cook for 2 to 3 minutes without browning. Gradually whisk in broth and cook until thick and smooth.

(2) Add carrots, peas and chicken, salt, peppers and tarragon. Mix well. Pour into two or three pans.

(3) In a bowl, stir together remaining flour, baking powder, 1 teaspoon of salt. Add ½ stick margarine. Beat eggs and milk and add to flour mixture. Spread over top of chicken mixture.

Bake at 375° for 25-30 minutes, until lightly brown.

CHICKEN CASSEROLE

20	cups cubed cooked chicken
1	2 lb. package elbow macaroni, cooked and drained
6	6 oz. jars sliced mushrooms
2	4 oz. jars pimentos, diced
2	large green peppers, chopped
2	large onions, chopped
4	10-3/4 oz. cans cream of celery soup, undiluted
4	10-3/4 oz. cans cream of mushroom soup, undiluted
2	lbs. processed American cheese, cubed
1/3	cup milk
4	teaspoons dried basil
2	teaspoons lemon pepper
2	cups crushed corn flakes
1/4	cup melted butter

Combine chicken, macaroni, mushrooms, pimentos, peppers and onions in a large bowl. Combine soups, milk, cheese, basil, lemon pepper and add to chicken mixture. Pour into greased pans. Cover and refrigerate overnight. Remove from refrigerator 30 minutes before baking. Combine corn flakes with butter, sprinkle over casserole. Cover and bake at 350° for 45 minutes. Uncover and bake 15 to 20 minutes, until bubbly.

Serves 45-50 (1 cup servings)

LASAGNA

4	lbs. ground beef
1	gallon spaghetti sauce
1	gallon diced tomatoes
4	15 oz. container of ricotta cheese
4	eggs, well beaten
1	cup parmesan cheese
4	teaspoons dried basil leaf, crushed
24	lasagna noodles
8	cups shredded mozzarella cheese

In Dutch oven, cook ground beef 4-6 minutes, until no longer pink, stir to break up into pea-sized bits. Drain drippings. Add spaghetti sauce and diced tomatoes. Stir. Set aside. In a separate bowl, combine ricotta cheese, eggs, parmesan cheese and basil. Spread 8 cups of beef mixture over bottom of two baking pans. In each pan, arrange 6 noodles in a single layer, pressing into the beef mixture. Spoon ricotta cheese mixture on top of noodles. Sprinkle 2 cups of mozzarella cheese over each pan. Spread four more cups of beef mixture over cheese layers in each pan. Arrange remaining six noodles per pan over beef mixture, pressing noodles tightly into beef mixture. Press remaining beef mixture over noodles.

Bake for 45 minutes in pre-heated oven at 375°, until noodles are tender. Spread remaining mozzarella over lasagna. Cover with tent of foil, let set for 15 minutes. Serves 38.

Since You're UP!

POTATO & GROUND BEEF CASSEROLE

36	lbs. ground chuck
35	lbs. potatoes., raw, thinly sliced
8	26 oz cans cream of mushroom soup
10	lbs onions, chopped
1	gallon milk
	salt and pepper

Brown ground beef. Mix beef and chopped onions and soup in six pans 15 x 28. Layer 1/3 of beef mixture into bottoms of pans. Cover with potatoes. Sprinkle with salt and pepper. Top with remaining beef mixture. Pour milk over top. Cover with foil. Bake for 90 minutes at 350°. Uncover and cook until potatoes are tender and top is brown, approximately 90 minutes more.

Serves 140.

POTATO SOUP

2/3	cup diced celery
2/3	cup diced carrots
2/3	cup diced onion
4	tablespoons margarine
4	tablespoons all-purpose flour
2	quarts milk
4	chicken bouillon cubes
4	tablespoons parsley
1	teaspoon salt
1/2	teaspoon cayenne pepper
12	medium potatoes, peeled and diced

Cook potatoes until tender and set aside. Cook celery, carrots and onion in margarine until tender. Stir in flour until smooth. Gradually add milk, cook and stir until thickened and bubbly. Add bouillon, parsley, salt and pepper. Simmer for 20 minutes, stirring. Add half of potatoes. Mash other half of potatoes and add to soup. Simmer for 20 minutes. Garnish with chives, cheese and/or bacon bits if desired.

Makes 1 gallon.

SWEET POTATO CASSEROLE

22	lbs. fresh sweet potatoes
2	lbs. margarine
1	cup orange juice concentrate
2	lbs. brown sugar
4	tablespoons grated orange rind

Cook potatoes until tender. Drain. Put into large bowl. Add margarine, orange juice concentrate, brown sugar and orange rind. Blend or mix until lump-free. Place into greased pan.

8	oz. margarine
28	oz. brown sugar
1	cup milk
8	oz. pecan pieces

Put margarine, brown sugar, milk and pecans into a saucepan. Bring to a boil and allow to cook until bubbly and mixture begins to thicken, approximately 4 minutes. Remove from heat and pour over potato mixture.

Bake at 400° for 20-30 minutes.

Serves 85

MACARONI & Cheese — 50 people

16 Tbsp Corn Starch
8 Tsp Salt
4 Tsp Dry Mustard
2 Tsp pepper
5 Qts Milk
2 stick Margarine
4 lb Cheese shredded
4 lb Elbow Macaroni

Combine starch, salt, mustard, pepper. Stir in milk until smooth. Add margarine, stirring constantly. Bring to boil over Med heat. Boil 1 minute. Remove from heat. Reserve 1 lb cheese for topping. Stir remaining cheese. Add elbows. Turn in greased pan. Sprinkle with Reserved Cheese. Bake uncovered 375° for 25 minutes until Hot & bubbly — Serves 50

MACARONI & CHEESE

16	tablespoons corn starch
8	teaspoons salt
4	teaspoons dry mustard
2	teaspoons pepper
5	quarts milk
2	sticks margarine
4	lbs. cheese, shredded
4	lbs. elbow macaroni

Cook macaroni until tender and set aside. Combine starch, salt, mustard and pepper. Stir in milk until smooth. Add margarine, stirring constantly, and bring to a boil over medium heat. Boil for one minute. Remove from heat. Add 3 lbs. cheese and cooked macaroni. Pour into greased pans. Sprinkle remaining cheese over top. Bake uncovered at 375° for 25 minutes.

Serves 50.

PASTA SALAD

1	lb. pasta
1	cup thinly sliced zucchini
1	cup broccoli florets
½	cup green pepper
½	cup red pepper
½	cup shredded carrots
½	cup pitted olives
	Salami, cut into thin strips
	Cheddar cheese, cut into thin strips

DRESSING:

1	cup undiluted Carnation milk
4-6	tablespoons vinegar
1	cup salad oil
1	teaspoon Italian seasoning
4	tablespoons grated parmesan cheese
1	tablespoon garlic salt

Combine dressing ingredients in jar and shake well. Chill before serving.

Serves 16.

BASIC RICE

8	cups rice
10	cups basic stock
½	cup very finely chopped onion
½	cup very finely chopped celery
1	stick melted margarine
2	teaspoons salt
½	teaspoon garlic powder

Combine all ingredients, mix well. Seal pan snugly with foil. Bake at 350° until rice is tender, approximately 70 minutes. Will stay hot for about 45 minutes.

Serves 40 (24 cups)

BROWN RICE

2	lbs. onions, chopped
2	lbs. butter
2	lbs. sliced mushrooms, drained
1	gallon beef consommé
4	oz. Worcestershire sauce
1	teaspoon black pepper
56	oz. rice

In a large pot, place onions, butter and mushrooms. Cook at a low simmer for 5 minutes or until onion begins to turn clear. Add consommé, Worcestershire sauce and pepper. Bring to a rapid boil. Add rice and cover. Turn down to medium-low heat and simmer 25 minutes.

Serves 68

RED BEANS & RICE

6	lbs red beans
18	cups water
6	large onions, chopped
12	cloves garlic, minced
3	large green peppers, chopped
3	large red peppers, chopped
1-1/2	lbs salt pork
3	cups dry red wine
1-1/2	cups chopped parsley
1-1/2	teaspoons oregano
3	tablespoons old bay seasoning
9	bay leaves
3	teaspoons celery seed
3	teaspoons salt
3	teaspoons pepper
1-1/2	teaspoons crushed red pepper
1-1/2	teaspoons ground red pepper
3	teaspoons hot sauce
6	lbs smoked sausage, cut into ½" pieces
6	11 oz. cans diced tomatoes & green chilies

Combine all ingredients except sausage and diced tomatoes and green chilies in a large pot. Bring to boil and cover. Reduce heat and simmer until tender. Add sausage and tomatoes/chilies and cook 30 minutes. Remove salt pork and bay leaves. Serve over rice.

Serves 45

HUSHPUPPY MIX

4	cups buttermilk, room temperature
2	lbs. salt
¼	cup sugar
8	oz. onions, chopped
2	eggs
4	cups flour
4	cups corn meal

In blender, put buttermilk, salt, sugar, onions and eggs. Blend for 30 seconds at high speed. Pour into medium sized bowl. Add flour and corn meal. Mix thoroughly with a wire whip. May be refrigerated. Drop into hot fryer for 4-5 minutes, until golden brown.

Makes 100

CORNBREAD

18	eggs
1-1/2	cups sugar
2/3	cup flour
13	cups buttermilk, room temperature
13	cups water
10	lbs corn meal
4	cups melted shortening
2	cups melted bacon fat

Preheat oven to 375°. Heat muffin tins or pans in oven for 15 minutes.

In a large bowl, put eggs, sugar and flour. Mix well with wire ship. Add buttermilk and water. Mix well with wire ship. Add corn meal and mix whit ship until smooth. Add melted shortening and bacon fat, and mixture will begin to thicken. Stir well until well blended. Allow batter to rest at room temperature for at least 15 minutes. Remove tins from oven and spray. Stir batter with wire ship to remix after rest period. Fill cups ¾ full. Bake 20 minutes or until golden brown.

Serves 130-140

BREAD PUDDING

3	quarts milk
10	eggs
½	cup vanilla
1-1/4	cups flour
2-1/2	cups sugar
2	cups raisins
46	oz day-old biscuits or bread
2	cups coconut

Spray bottom of a pot with cooking spray. Pour in milk and heat to 170°. In a bowl, combine eggs, vanilla, flour and sugar. Mix thoroughly and add to milk. Cook until consistency is custard-like, stirring constantly with wire ship. Grate biscuits or bread and pour into pan. Add raisins and coconut to bread mixture and mix thoroughly. Pour pudding mixture into bread mixture. Stir thoroughly. Bake for 10 minutes at 375°.

Serves 35

ICING FOR BREAD PUDDING

1-1/2	cups milk
1-1/2	cups sugar
1-1/2	cups coconut

Combine ingredients and bring mixture to a boil. Cook, stirring constantly, until mixture thickens. Pour over already-baked pudding. Serve hot or cold.

Since You're UP!

APPLE COBBLER

6	cups biscuit mix
6-3/4	cups sugar
1-1/2	cups milk
1	cup raisins
6	eggs
4-1/2	cups apple jelly
3	teaspoons orange extract
¾	cup margarine, melted
3	20 oz can apple pie filling
¾	teaspoon cinnamon

Combine biscuit mix, 6 cups sugar, milk, eggs, cinnamon and margarine. Mix well. Spread in two 11 x 17 pans. Spoon apple pie filling over batter and sprinkle with raisins. Melt 3 cups of apple jelly and pour over batter. Bake at 350° for 50 minutes, until golden brown. Combine remaining jelly and orange extract. Melt, mix well and pour and spread evenly over hot cobbler. Sprinkle with remaining sugar.

Since You're UP!

FRIED APPLES

1	#10 can sliced apples (unpeeled)
1-1/4	cups sugar
2	teaspoons ground cinnamon
½	lb margarine

Pour apples into baking dish. Put sugar and cinnamon in bowl and mix until cinnamon is evenly distributed. Pour mixture over apples. Cut margarine and dot the top of apples. Bake at 300° for 20 minutes. Remove and stir gently. Return to oven for 10 minutes.

Serves 25

APPLE PIE

4	unbaked pie shells
1	#10 can unpeeled sliced apples
1	cup sugar
8	tablespoons flour
4	teaspoons ground cinnamon

Preheat oven to 300°. Empty apples into a large bowl. Add sugar, flour and cinnamon. Mix gently. Empty mixture into pie shells. Sprinkle streusel topping (below) onto mixture. Bake 50 minutes.

STREUSEL TOPPING FOR APPLE PIE

8	oz. margarine
2	cups firmly packed brown sugar
2	cups flour
2	cups pecan pieces

Using pastry blade attachment, mix margarine, sugar, pecans and flour together until margarine is pea-sized. Makes topping for four pies.

Since You're UP!

PAPPY-LICIOUS

One of the fondest cooking memories that I have with Pappy is one of my actually watching rather than participating. It was usually in the winter time when Pappy would make the family peanut brittle. It fascinated me because of the way it was prepared. The melting of the wax and the pouring of hot liquid candy into the pans over the peanuts always kept my attention until Pappy said it was ok to break apart. Looking back, the best part of making peanut brittle is remembering the joy on Pappy's face when he looked at us enjoying another culinary delight.

-Robert Ward

PAPPY'S PAN PEANUT BRITTLE

1-1/2	cups sugar
½	cup Karo syrup
1/16	square paraffin
2	cups roasted peanuts (shelled)
2	tablespoons soda

Combine the sugar, Karo and paraffin in a large pot and boil to 300°. When boiling reduce to medium heat for 12 minutes stirring constantly. Add soda and stir until dissolved. (Soda may foam). Spread quickly on oiled/buttered pans containing a layer of roasted peanuts. Let cool throughout before breaking apart.

PAPPY'S PINEAPPLE CHERRY DELIGHT

1	8 oz. sour cream
1	12 oz. cool whip
1	can crushed pineapple (16 oz.)
1	can cherry pie filling
1	can Eagle brand condensed milk
1	cup chopped nuts
½	teaspoon lemon juice

Mix all ingredients together and chill before serving.

HOT FUDGE SAUCE

3   cups powdered sugar
7   tablespoons cocoa or 3 sq. choc.
1   stick butter
1   14 oz. can condensed milk
1 ½   teaspoon vanilla

Melt butter and cocoa or chocolate. Add sugar. Gradually add milk and blend. Bring to a boil over medium heat. Boil 8 minutes and then add vanilla.

BRENDA'S CHERRY TOPPED CHEESE PIE

1	8 oz. package softened cream cheese
½	cup sugar
2	cups cool whip
1	cup canned cherry pie filling
1	unbaked 9" graham cracker crust

Beat together softened cream cheese and sugar until creamy. Blend cool whip. Pour into unbaked 9" graham cracker crust. Top with canned cherry pie filling. Chill 3 hours.

COCONUT PIE

½	stick melted butter
1	cup sugar
1/3	cup buttermilk
2	eggs
1	teaspoon vanilla
1	cup coconut

Mix all ingredients together and pour into an uncooked pie shell. Bake 30 to 40 minutes at 325°.

BUTTERMILK LEMON PIE

Pie:
1	cup sugar
½	cup all purpose flour
2	cups buttermilk
½	cup water
3	eggs yolks, lightly beaten
6	tablespoons fresh squeezed lemon juice
2	tablespoons butter or margarine

Meringue:
3	egg whites
6	tablespoons sugar
9	inch pastry shell, baked

In a large saucepan, combine sugar and flour. Gradually stir in buttermilk and water until smooth. Cook and stir over medium heat until thickened and bubbly, about 4 minutes. Reduce heat. Cook and stir 2 minutes longer. Remove from the heat. Stir a small amount of hot filling into egg yolks; return all to the pan, stirring constantly. Bring to a gentle boil; cook and stir 2 minutes longer. Remove from the heat; stir in lemon juice and butter until butter is melted. Keep warm. In small mixing bowl, beat the egg whites on medium speed until soft peaks form. Gradually beat in sugar, 1 tablespoon at a time on high just until stiff peaks form and sugar is dissolved. Pour the hot filling into pastry shell. Spread meringue evenly over hot filling, sealing edges to crust. Bake at 350° for 15 minutes or until meringue is golden brown. Cool on a wire rack for 1 hour and refrigerate 5 hours before serving.

Since You're UP!

SALLY'S BANANA PUDDING

1	box vanilla wafer cookies
1	large container of whipped topping
2	pkgs. Instant vanilla pudding
3	cups milk
6 – 7	bananas

Combine whipped topping, instant vanilla pudding and milk until well blended. In a large serving bowl, layer wafer cookies on the bottom. Then layer sliced bananas on the wafer cookies. Add a layer of pudding mixture. Repeat layering of wafers, bananas, and pudding mixture. Refrigerate and serve cold.

TOPPING FOR APPLE OR PEACH CRISP

2	sticks butter
2	cups flour
2	cups sugar
2	teaspoons cinnamon

Melt butter and set aside to cool. Stir flour, sugar and cinnamon, add cooled melted butter and mix with fingers until mixture resembles big crumbs. Sprinkle over apples or peaches (in juice). Bake at 350° for 20 to 30 minutes.

APPLE DUMPLINGS

1	stick butter
1	cup sugar
1	cup orange juice
1	can crescent rolls
1-2	Granny Smith apples

Place butter, sugar and orange juice in a saucepan and bring to a boil. Peel and core apples, cut into squares. Wrap each apple with dough. Pour sauce over apples. Bake at 350° until brown.

PECAN TARTS

2	tablespoons melted margarine
½	cup sugar
¼	teaspoon salt
2	beaten eggs
1	teaspoon vanilla
1	cup dark Karo
	Pecan halves

Mix all ingredients except pecans and pour into unbaked tart shells. Top with pecan halves. Bake at 350° for 40-45 minutes. Makes 8 tarts or 1 pie.

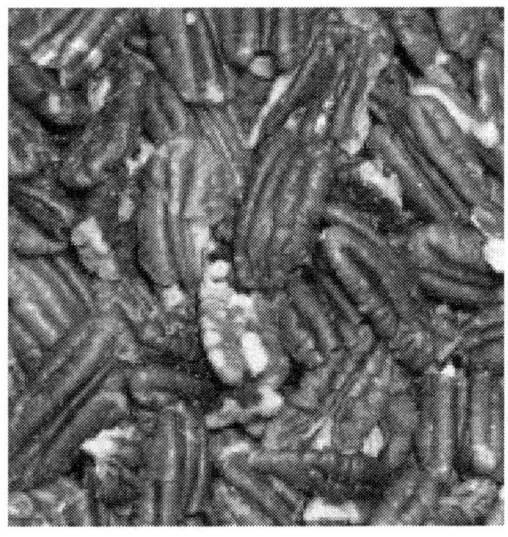

APPLE RAISIN SNACK BARS

1	package (2-layer size) spice cake mix
1/4	cup Miracle Whip
2	eggs
1/2	cup chopped apple
1/2	cup chopped raisins

Blend cake mix, Miracle Whip and eggs until well blended. Stir in apples and raisins. Spread in 13 x 9 baking pan. Bake at 350° for 25-30 minutes.

Frosting:

3-1/2	cups powdered sugar
1	stick margarine, softened
2	tablespoons milk
1	teaspoon vanilla

Blend all ingredients with electric mixer until light and fluffy.

Makes 15 servings.

Since You're UP!

THELMA'S APPLESAUCE CAKE

2/3	cups butter (1/2 lb)
2	cups white sugar
2	teaspoons cinnamon
1	teaspoon cloves
½	teaspoon nutmeg
¼	teaspoon salt
2	teaspoons vanilla
2	cups thick applesauce
2	teaspoons soda dissolved in a little warm water
4	cups flour
1	package dates
1	package raisins
1	cup walnuts or pecans
2	pieces candied pineapple
½	piece candied citron
1	package figs
1	cup pecans
¼	lb. candied cherries

Combine butter, sugar, cinnamon, cloves and nutmeg. Mix applesauce with salt and vanilla and add to mixture. Add other ingredients, adding flour one cup at a time. Bake at 325-350° for approximately 2-1/2 hours.

LEDDIE'S FRUITCAKE

1	lb cherries (red and green)
1	lb pineapple (red and green)
1-1/2	boxes raisins
1	jar mince meat
1	qt. preserves (fig recommended)
1	can apple sauce
1	lb margarine
12	eggs
	nuts
3	cups sugar
5	cups self-rising flour
	cinnamon
½	cup orange juice
1	small package dates

Cut up fruit and nuts and mix. Add cinnamon, then sugar. Melt margarine and put into mixture and mix. Add orange juice and mix. Add flour and mix well with hands. Cut brown paper to fit bottom of pan. Grease bottom of pan and paper well. Fill pans about ¾ full and bake at 250° for 3 hours or until done.

SUE'S COCONUT CAKE

1	cup sugar
8	oz. sour cream
2	packages frozen coconut, thawed
1	small pack Cool Whip or Winn-Dixie topping

Several hours before preparing cake (day before is ok), stir together sugar, sour cream and 1-1/2 packages of coconut. Store in refrigerator in air-tight container until ready to ice cake.

1	two-layer Duncan Hines yellow cake or white cake

Bake layers separately. Cool thoroughly.

Add whipped topping to sugar-sour cream-coconut mixture. Spread between layers and on top and side of cake. Sprinkle remaining coconut over top of cake.

Store cake in airtight container in refrigerator.

MOUND CAKE

1	cup sugar
12	large marshmallows
1	cup milk
2	packages cookie coconut
1	Duncan Hines Swiss chocolate cake mix
1	can Double Dutch chocolate frosting

Mix sugar, marshmallows and milk until marshmallows are melted. Add coconut, cook for 5 minutes. Set aside to cool.

Prepare cake ix according to directions and bake in 3 layers. Cool cake.

Stack cake with coconut filling between layers. Frost with chocolate icing.

CREAMY FROSTING FOR VANILLA WAFER CAKE

2/3	cup Carnation milk
2/3	cups sugar
1/4	cups margarine

Combine ingredients. Boil for 3 minutes. Let cool, then beat until consistency is suitable for spreading (about 5-10 minutes). Spread on cake

BUTTER CREAM FROSTING

1/2	cup shortening
1/2	cup butter or margarine, softened
1	teaspoon vanilla extract
4	cups confectioner's sugar
3	tablespoons milk

Cream shortening and butter in mixing bowl. Add vanilla. Gradually beat in sugar. Add milk, beat until light and fluffy. Frost cake!

TOPPING FOR GERMAN CHOCOLATE CAKE

1 ½	cups sugar
¾	cup butter
1	large can evaporated milk
1½	teaspoon vanilla
2	eggs, whole, beaten well
1-1/3	cups coconut
1	cup pecans, chopped

In a medium saucepan, combine first five ingredients. Cook low heat until thin, remove from heat. Stir in coconut and pecans. Cool for 15 minutes. Spread on cake.

PINEAPPLE CREAM FROSTING

½	cup butter or margarine
1	lb confectioner's sugar
1	8 oz package cream cheese
1	teaspoon vanilla
3-4	tablespoons drained crushed pineapple

Combine ingredients. Spread on cake.

Since You're UP!

BANANA BREAD

1/3	cup shortening
2/3	cup sugar
2	eggs, slightly beaten
1-3/4	cups self-rising flour
1	cup mashed ripe bananas

Beat shortening until creamy and glossy. Add sugar and beat until fluffy. Add eggs, beat until thick and pale lemon yellow in color. Stir in flour, adding alternately with bananas. Blend thoroughly. Bake at 350° for 60 to 70 minutes.

SNOWBALL COOKIES

1	cup (2 sticks) butter
6	tablespoons confectioner's sugar
2	cups plain flour
2	teaspoons vanilla
2	cups pecans, finely chopped

Cream sugar with butter. Add other ingredients and mix until desired consistency. Chill dough slightly. Pinch off pieces for cookies. Lightly spray pan. Bake at 300° for 20 minutes. Roll in confectioner's sugar while warm.

STRAWBERRY PUDDING

3	10 oz packages frozen strawberries
1	small package strawberry gelatin
2	small boxes instant vanilla pudding
3	cups cold sweet milk
1	8 oz container whipped topping
1	8 oz container sour cream
1	large box vanilla wafers

Mix strawberries and gelatin together and heat. Let cool. Blend pudding and milk until thick. Fold in whipped topping and sour cream. Layer pan or dish with vanilla wafers, then a layer of pudding mixture, then a layer of strawberries. Repeat the three layers in that order. Chill.

CHOCOLATE FUDGE

2	sticks margarine
4	cups sugar
1	can milk
2	packages chocolate chips
1	jar marshmallow cream
1	cup nuts (optional)

Mix chocolate chips and marshmallow cream in a bowl. Mix butter, sugar and milk and boil for 9 minutes. Pour mixture over chocolate chips and marshmallow mix. Beat with wooden spoon until glossy. Pour into container. Refrigerate. Add nuts if desired. Cut into squares.

COCONUT CHOCOLATE SQUARES

2	12 oz bags coconut
1	lb confectioner's sugar
½	cup margarine
1	teaspoon vanilla
1	can condensed milk (Borden's recommended)
½	bar thick wax or 1 bar thin wax
1	12 oz bag semi-sweet chocolate chips (pure chocolate)

Mix coconut, sugar, margarine, vanilla and milk. Pour into two long Pyrex dishes. Let chill overnight in refrigerator. Melt wax and chocolate over low heat and stir to blend thoroughly. Cut coconut mixture into squares, dip into chocolate. Cool on wax paper. May be chilled in freezer for 15 minutes if you're in a hurry!

PEANUT BUTTER EASTER EGGS

2	sticks margarine, melted
12	oz. crunchy peanut butter (extra crunchy)
1	box confectioner's sugar
1	small can coconut
2	cups graham cracker crumbs
1	teaspoon vanilla
1	large bag chocolate chips
¼	piece paraffin

Combine margarine, peanut butter, sugar, coconut, graham cracker crumbs and vanilla. Form into eggs. Melt chocolate and paraffin. Dip "eggs" into chocolate.

CANDIED PECANS

1	egg white
1	teaspoon vanilla
¾	cup light brown sugar
	Pecan halves

Beat egg white until stiff. Add brown sugar a little at a time, then add vanilla. Dip pecans in mixture. Arrange on cookie sheet. Bake 30 minutes at 250°. Turn off oven. Do not open oven door. Leave until cool.

PAPPY'S COOL LEMON PIE

2	egg whites
1	tablespoon sugar
2	egg yolks
1	can condensed milk (large)
4	lemons (juice only-to individual taste)
2	cups whipped topping
1	cooked pie crust

In a large mixing bowl, combine egg yolks, condensed milk, and lemon juice. Add whipped topping a little at a time. Once mixed, set aside. Beat egg whites while adding sugar until peaks are formed. Pour pie mixture into cooked pie crust. Spread beaten egg whites over pie mixture while making a pattern with spoon. Put under boiler until egg white topping is golden brown. Do not leave unattended as egg whites burn easily. Refrigerate for a while, then serve.

BANANA-APPLE SURPRIZE

bananas
apples
butter
cinnamon
brown sugar
honey

Amount of ingredients depends on how much you want to prepare. Take a baking pan and layer the bottom with all ingredients except bananas and apples. Then take the bananas and apples and slice or chop or chunk or a combination. Put the fruit in the baking pan and repeat butter, cinnamon, brown sugar and honey on the top of the fruit. Put in preheated oven 350° and bake 20 – 30 minutes. Serve warm with main meal or serve warm with ice cream as a dessert.

Since You're UP!

INDEX

A

APPLE COBBLER	92
APPLE DUMPLINGS	102
APPLE PIE	94
APPLE RAISIN SNACK BARS	104

B

BBA SAUCE	13
BBQ SLAW	34
BACKALLEY BRUNSWICK STEW	53
BAKED BEANS	21
BANANA-APPLE SURPRIZE	116
BANANA BREAD	111
BANANA PUDDING	101
BASIC RICE	87
BEEF STEW	73
BEEF TIPS	75
BLACK BEAN DIP	9
BREAD PUDDING	91
BRENDA'S CHERRY TOPPED CHEESE PIE	99
BROCCOLI & CAULIFLOWER DRESSING	32
BROCCOLI NOODLE SLAW	34
BROWN RICE	87
BUTTER CREAM FROSTING	109
BUTTERMILK LEMON PIE	100

C

CANDIED PECANS	114
CABBAGE A LA PAPPY	24
CHEESEBURGER PIE	50
CHERRY TOPPED CHEESE PIE	99
CHICKEN CASSEROLE	79
CHICKEN & DUMPLINGS	62, 63
CHICKEN & NOODLES	60
CHICKEN PIE DELUXE	78
CHICKEN & RICE CASSEROLE	68

Since You're UP!

CHICKEN & ROTELLE SALAD WITH PESTO DRESSING	61
CHILI FOR A MULE	25
CHOCOLATE FUDGE	112
CHOW-CHOW-CHOW-DOWN RELISH	27
COATED BAKED CHICKEN OR FISH	67
COCONUT CHOCOLATE SQUARES	113
COCONUT PIE	99
CORNBREAD	90
CORNMEAL CREPES	20
CORN RELISH	29
CRABMEAT FILLING	19
CREAM OF BROCCOLI SOUP	38
CREAMY FROSTING FOR VANILLA WAFER CAKE	109

D

DEVILED EGG FILLING	17
DIRTY RICE	20
DRAYTON STREET SOUP	37

F

FETTUCCINE	57
FIESTA CREPES EN CASSEROLE	49
FRIED APPLES	93
FRIED APPLE PIES	5
FRIED OKRA	23
FRIED SQUASH	24

G

GARDEN VEGETABLE BEEF SOUP	41
GINGER CHICKEN	65
GLAZE FOR MEATLOAF	74
GRAPE JUICE WINE	16
GRAPE WINE	16

H

HAMBURGER SALAMI	47
HORSERADISH HAM FILLING	5
HOT FUDGE SAUCE	98
HUSHPUPPIES	4, 89

Since You're UP!

I
ICING FOR BREAD PUDDING　　　　　　　91

J
JAPANESE CHICKEN WINGS　　　　　　　66
JUST MARINARA SAUCE　　　　　　　　　69

L
LASAGNA　　　　　　　　　　　　　　　80
LAUREN'S GRAVY　　　　　　　　　　　45
LEDDIE'S FRUITCAKE　　　　　　　　　106
LINDA'S LASAGNA　　　　　　　　　　　56

M
MACARONI & CHEESE　　　　　　　　　　85
MAC-N-CHEESE CROCKPOT　　　　　　　51
MAMMY'S MEATLOAF　　　　　　　　　　50
MARINATED VEGETABLES　　　　　　　　36
MEATLOAF　　　　　　　　　　　　　　74
MOO GOO GAI PAN　　　　　　　　　　　64
MORE CHICKEN & DUMPLINGS　　　　　　63
MOUND CAKE　　　　　　　　　　　　　108

O
ORANGE GELATIN SALAD　　　　　　　　15

P
PAPPY'S CANDIED SWEET POTATOES　　　23
PAPPY'S CASSEROLE　　　　　　　　　　46
PAPPY'S CHILI IN A POT　　　　　　　　70
PAPPY'S COOL LEMON PIE　　　　　　　115
PAPPY'S HOMEMADE BBQ SAUCE　　　　　13
PAPPY'S HOT PEPPER SAUCE　　　　　　30
PAPPY'S OLD TIME RELISH　　　　　　　26
PAPPY'S PAN PEANUT BRITTLE　　　　　97
PAPPY'S PARMESAN BITES　　　　　　　　7
PAPPY'S PASTA SALAD　　　　　　　　　35
PAPPY'S PICKLE HOT PEPPER　　　　　　28
PAPPY'S PINEAPPLE CHERRY DELIGHT　　97

Since You're UP!

PAPPY'S PORK HASH	52
PAPPY'S SALAD DRESSING	33
PAPPY'S SWEET & SPICY MUSTARD	31
PAPPY'S TATER SOUP	39
PARTY BEEF CASSEROLE	76
PASTA CARBONARA	59
PASTA SALAD	86
PEANUT BUTTER EASTER EGGS	114
PECAN TARTS	103
PICKLED BEETS	15
PICKLED PEACHES	15
PINEAPPLE CREAM FROSTING	110
POTATO GROUND BEEF CASSEROLE	81
POTATO SOUP	82

R

RAISIN SAUCE	29
RED BEANS & RICE	55, 88
RISE-N-SHINE BISCUITS WITH LAUREN'S GRAVY	45
ROAST PORK	51

S

SALLY'S BANANA PUDDING	101
SALMON CANAPES	19
SLAW DRESSING	33
SLOPPY JOES	77
SNOWBALL COOKIES	111
SPAGHETTI & MEATBALLS	58
SPEEDY CASSEROLE	48
SPINACH & BLACKEYED PEA SALAD	18
SPINACH DIP	9
SPINACH SQUARES	6
SQUASH CASSEROLE	22
STRAWBERRY PUDDING	112
STREUSEL TOPPING FOR APPLE PIE	94
SUE'S COCONUT CAKE	107
SWEET CHOW CHOW	28
SWEET POTATO CASSEROLE	83
SWEET & SOUR SAUCE FOR MOO GOO GAI PAN	64

Since You're UP!

T
TACO SEASONING	31
TATER-N-BEEF CASSEROLE	47
THE MULE SANDWICH	25
THELMA'S APPLESAUCE CAKE	105
TOPPING FOR APPLE OR PEACH CRISP	110
TOPPING FOR GERMAN CHOCOLATE CAKE	110
TURKEY CHEESEBALL	8

V
VEGETABLE SOUP	40
VENISON JERKY	4
VENISON SALAMI	3

W
WHITE TRASH	7

www.ingramcontent.com/pod-product-compliance
Lightning Source LLC
Chambersburg PA
CBHW032138040426
42449CB00005B/296